# Deploying a Mobile Application to the App Store with Ionic Capacitor

*How you can publish any web application to the App Store in about an hour*

*By*

*Michael D. Callaghan*

walkingriver.com

Twitter: @WalkingRiver

# Table of Contents

# Introduction

These days, it seems that everyone wants to build mobile apps. Even web developers.

The bad news is that there are too many technologies involved and the process can be somewhat convoluted. Apple certainly does its best to complicate things.

The good news is that you do not have to ignore standard Web technologies such as HTML, JavaScript, and TypeScript.

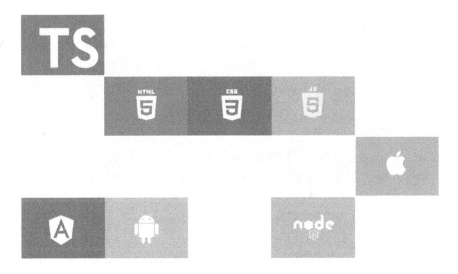

If you are a web developer and want to build mobile apps, but you do not want to take the time to learn native mobile development technologies, then this book is for you.

I will show you not only how easy it is to build your own app, but also how fun it can be.

You will see how you can quickly take your existing Web application and deploy it to the Apple App Store and make it available to millions of iOS devices.

Take a look at these apps.

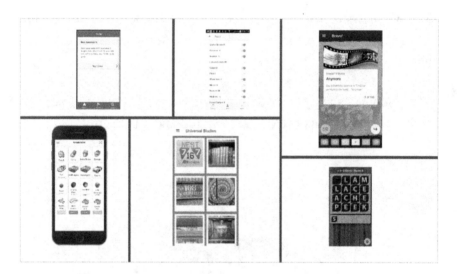

Each one of them is a Web application wrapped in an Xcode project and deployed to the App Store. And these are just the few that I built myself. Almost a third of all apps in the Apple App Store are built with Web technologies. How amazing is that?

Now it is your turn. Get your favorite Web app ready and join me on this fast-paced journey to enter the world of mobile application development.

**I do not want to waste your time!**

This book is about one thing and one thing only. Getting your web application onto the Apple App Store, where it will then be available to the tens of millions of iOS users all over the world.

In this book, I will show you how to get a web application prepared and deployed to the Apple App Store.

How are you going to do that? With Capacitor from Ionic.

Capacitor is a modern piece of technology that will allow you to wrap an existing web application in an Xcode project and then deploy it to the Apple App Store. This book will cover the basics you need to take one of your own web apps (or you can use one of mine if you prefer) and turn it into a function iOS app.

When you are finished, you should be able to replicate the process with every web app you want to put in the hands of iOS owners everywhere.

# Before You Begin

## Prerequisites

There are some prerequisites you must have before you begin.

 You need a Mac; which I assume you have if you are reading this; if not, feel free to follow along. But you will not be able to deploy anything.

You need to be a registered Apple developer. I will not go over everything required to get set up as an Apple developer, but you can sign up at https://developer.apple.com

 And finally, you need Xcode, which you can download from the Mac App Store.

## Demo Application

If you do not have your own web application and simply want to follow along, you are free to clone either of the applications I have here.

https://github.com/walkingriver/at10dance-angular

https://github.com/walkingriver/at10dance-react

Simply clone one of these repositories and then execute

```
npm install
```

inside the generated folder. You will need Node 8 or later, which you can find at http://nodejs.org.

If you decide to clone one of my repos, use one the following blocks of commands to get you up and running quickly:

## Clone and Build the Angular Version

```
git clone https://github.com/walkingriver/at10dance-angular.git
npm install
npm run build
```

## Clone and Build the React Version

```
git clone https://github.com/walkingriver/at10dance-react.git
npm install
npm run build
```

Note: These two repositories are for the demo application from my Ionic "Idea to App Store" series.

# Creating an Xcode Project

The first thing you must do is create a project that you can open in Xcode from an existing web application. This will become the basis of the application you eventually deploy to Apple.

The best way to create either an iOS Project from any Web app is by adding Capacitor to your project. Sure, you could use Cordova, but that is so last decade.

If you want the best experience with the least amount of friction, trust me, you will want to use Capacitor.

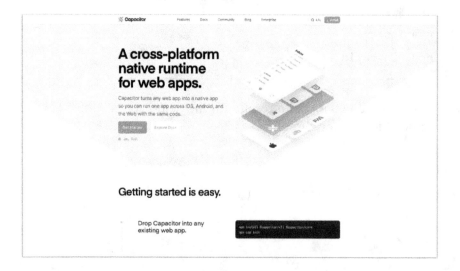

Capacitor ([https://capacitorjs.com](https://capacitorjs.com)) is a technology from Ionic, which does not actually require Ionic. In fact, nothing you are about to see or do requires Ionic.

## Install Capacitor into the Project

To use Capacitor, you must have some code built already, which you should have done at the end of the last chapter.

At this point, you have a complete Web application inside of the build folder.

Enter the following commands to install and initialize Capacitor.

```
npm install @capacitor/cli @capacitor/core
npx cap init [name] [id]
```

# Create Xcode Project

The next thing, now that you have Capacitor, is to install the iOS platform, which will create an Xcode project for you automatically.

And you do that with this command:

```
npx cap add ios
```

In case you are not familiar with it, NPX is Node's way of executing a command that may not be installed on your machine, but possibly those that exist only on the Node registry.

One of the benefits of NPX is that can execute node package binaries that are not in your system directory but installed somewhere inside of your node_modules folder.

And because Capacitor is installed locally, it is not on your normal command path.

For more information about NPX, see this article:
https://blog.npmjs.org/post/162869356040/introducing-npx-an-npm-package-runner

# Open the Xcode Project

Next you will want to open the project in Xcode itself. You can do that with Capacitor also, using the command:

```
npx cap open ios
```

This will launch Xcode with the project.

Now see if you can run it. Choose any of the simulated devices in the dropdown. Select a device and click the Play button.

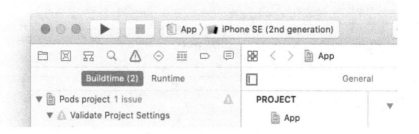

If you look at the bottom area of Xcode, you can see the console. Any console or log messages that are happening or any errors that are running, any errors that occur while you are running will appear here.

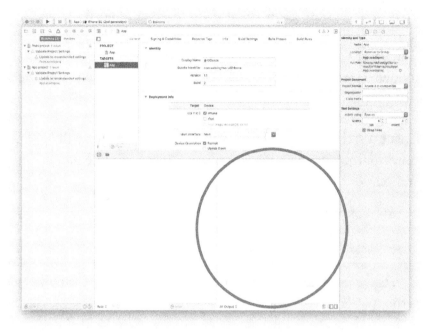

Play around with the running application and make sure it works as expected.

That is as far as you need to dig into Capacitor for now. It has done the hard part for you.

## Convenience Script (postbuild)

Now that you have an iOS project for the demo app, a couple of things you want to do quickly. And again, everything you do here applies for all the different types of applications.

The first is to open the package.json file in the project and add a script that will make some of this a little easier.

If you make any changes at all to the web app, you must rebuild it, and then you must synchronize those changes with the Capacitor project.

To do that, you are going to make use of npm's "post" scripts.

Whenever you have a script that starts with the word "post" followed by another word, npm will run that script right after the first script.

Create a script in package.json called "postbuild" that will synchronize with the Capacitor project. Place it inside the "scripts" section.

```
"scripts": {
  "postbuild": "cap sync",
```

Because it is named "postbuild" it will run right after the build script.

This script is simply calling capacitor's sync command, which will automatically copy the built artifacts to all the Capacitor projects that you have, with whatever platforms that are installed.

Give that a try. Run the command:

```
npm run build
```

NPM will build the application. Then it will immediately synchronize with Capacitor. It may have even updated some native iOS dependencies.

# Run on Device

Next you need to get the application running on an actual device. You just ran it on the simulator, but that is not where you need to be to get this thing onto the App Store.

What you see below is that Xcode is not very happy right now because before I took this screenshot, I removed my developer account from Xcode. I have also told it not to automatically manage signing.

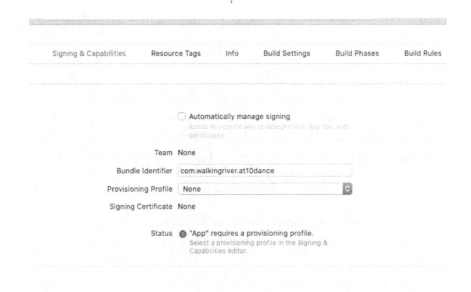

But you want to do that, so click the button to have it automatically manage signing. Xcode will not like that unless you are already logged in with your Apple developer account.

If not, then it still is not going to work.

Why?

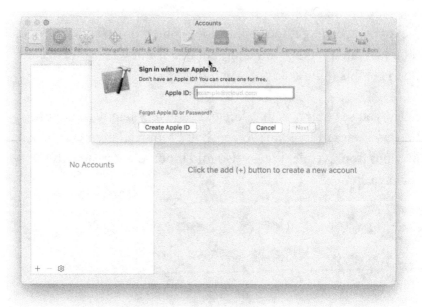

Because you need a development team, so log into your Apple development account. Then click the button to "Automatically manage signing." Select a team and update the bundle identifier to something unique.

Xcode should select the right Provisioning Profile and Signing Certificate for you. Now when you build the project, it should succeed.

## Using QuickTime to Mirror an iPhone

If you have not yet done so, connect your iPhone to your Mac.

I want to show you a cool little feature that you may not be aware of. Launch QuickTime Player, which will let you enable a movie recording to mirror your iPhone to your Mac.

Once you have launched QuickTime Player, select the File | New Movie Recording and then select your iPhone.

You will not have any control over the iPhone from your computer, but you can you can simply control it from your phone as you normally would.

## Run App on the Device

By now Xcode should be building your project successfully. But you did not run it yet.

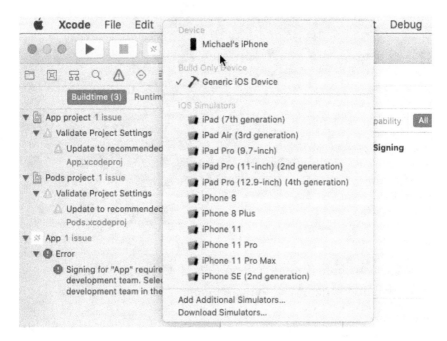

Select your device you just connected in the dropdown and press the Play icon.

What you should see first is the default Capacitor icon as the application is deployed to the phone.

Next, the application will launch with the default Capacitor splash screen. We will take care of those soon.

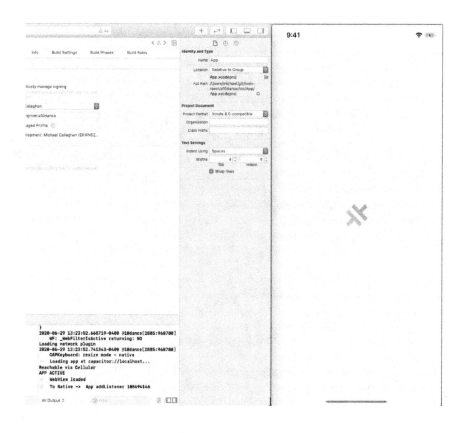

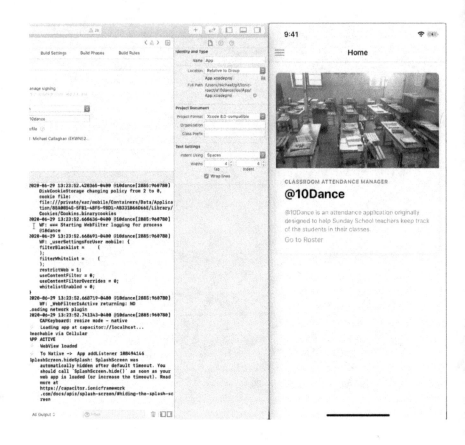

You can see the application's console log scrolling at the bottom of the Xcode window.

How cool is that?

# Creating the App Store App

The next major step is getting the built application to the App Store.

But first, you need a place to put it.

You need to go to Appstore Connect to create the application before you can upload it.

To do that, open a browser to https://appstoreconnect.apple.com and log in with your Apple developer account.

Once you are logged in, it shows you all the applications that you have currently got on the App Store.

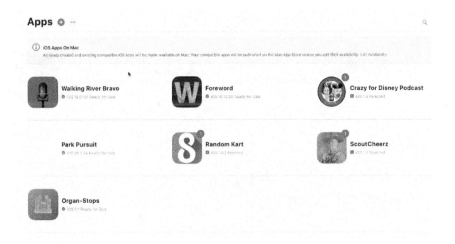

This is my Apps list. You can see a few of them with the red badges and the word "Rejected" next to them. There are many reasons for this: Apple policy violations, potential copyright issues, or even value judgments by Apple.

I am not going to go into any more details here. Just be aware that Apple is known to reject applications, sometimes for bizarre reasons.

## Create New Application Bundle

To create a new application, simply click the blue plus icon and select "New App."

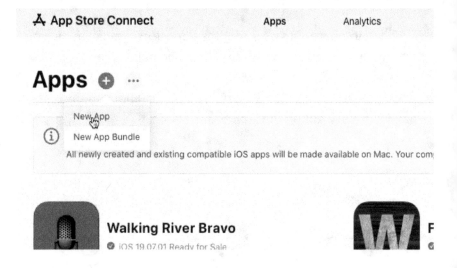

*Bundle ID*

On the popup window that appears, click on "Certificates, Identifiers & Profiles."

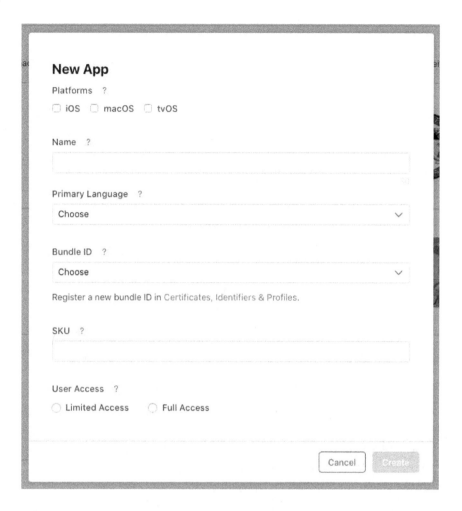

On the next screen, enter a simple description for the ID. This is what will appear in the Bundle ID dropdown on the previous page.

Select an Explicit Bundle ID and enter the exact same string you entered in Xcode.

# Certificates, Identifiers & Profiles

‹ All Identifiers

### Register an App ID

| Platform | App ID Prefix |
| --- | --- |
| iOS, macOS, tvOS, watchOS | WJ94B2HA7U (Team ID) |

Description

A10Dance

You cannot use special characters such as @, &, *, ', ", -, .

Bundle ID  ● Explicit      ○ Wildcard

com.walkingriver.a10dance|

We recommend using a reverse-domain name style string (i.e.,
com.domainname.appname). It cannot contain an asterisk (*).

### Capabilities

| ENABLED | NAME |
| --- | --- |
| ☐ | 🔍 Access WiFi Information |
| ☐ | ✅ App Attest |
| ☐ | ⊞ App Groups |
| ☐ | 💳 Apple Pay Payment Processing |
| ☐ | 🌐 Associated Domains |

## *Application Capabilities*

Apple also wants to know what iOS features that you are planning to use in this application. In my demo app, I am not planning for any of these, so I left them all blank.

Scroll through the list and select only those capabilities you know your app will need.

When you are finished, click, the Continue button.

# Create New App

Unfortunately, you may need to start the new app process again. If so, click New App… again.

Look at the Bundle ID drop down and you should see your new ID.

Complete the form as you did before using this example if necessary.

There is no need to limit your users. That is beyond this tutorial. Anyone who wants to can download it. Click Create, which will return you to the Apps page.

At this point, you can stop. There is a lot more to be done here, but the purpose of doing this was simply to get an app created so that you can upload the application.

# Upload to AppStore Connect

In this chapter, your goal is going to be uploading the application to Apple. You will not do anything with it yet.

I just want to show you how to create a signed application bundle and upload it to Apple.

Open the project in Xcode again.

I will explain one of the first mistakes I made, so you do not have to suffer the pain I did.

Imagine you are using the iPhone Simulator to run the app.

The first mistake I made is not knowing that Archive is the command to use to create the signed bundle.

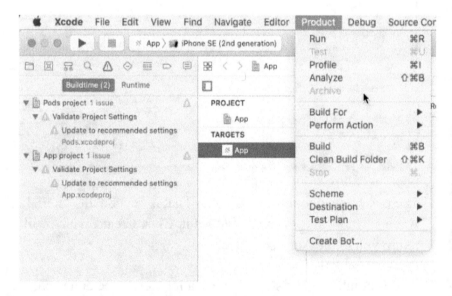

The second mistake was not being able to figure out why the Archive command is almost always disabled.

The reason is the device specified, the active scheme as it is called, is a simulated device.

Earlier, when I first showed this running an Xcode, I used the iPhone SE simulator and now you do not have any iPhone connected to the Mac.

What can you do about it? You have two choices. You can either plug in a real device or you can simply set the device to Generic.

That act alone will enable archive. Go ahead and do one of those two things now.

## Archive and Create the App Bundle

Now, select the Archive command from the Product menu.

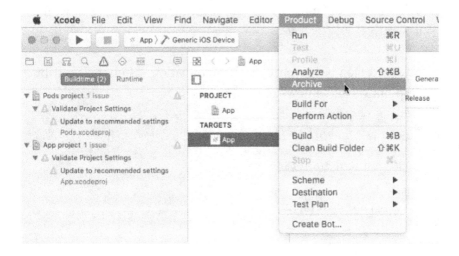

At this point, assuming you took the Capacitor application, built it and ran it on your iPhone, logged into your Apple account and

everything is being automatically managed, all the signing, etc…
in theory, this should just work.

It can take quite some time to build everything.

Hopefully, after a few minutes, the build succeeded and now.

# Distribute App

Xcode next wants to know what you want to do with your archive.

Notice that the application name is still App. Probably not where
you want to leave it, nor do you want version 1.0. For now, that is
not critical.

The next step is to distribute the application. Click the Distribute
App button and a new screen appears.

### Select a Method of Distribution

There are four choices here.

- App Store Connect
- Ad Hoc
- Enterprise
- Development

Select a method of distribution:

- ● App Store Connect
  Distribute on TestFlight and the App Store.
- ○ Ad Hoc
  Install on designated devices.
- ○ Enterprise
  Distribute to your organization.
- ○ Development
  Distribute to members of your team.

?

Cancel                                    Previous    Next

I recommend accepting the default (App Store Connect) because, quite frankly, you probably do not want to use ad hoc to install on arbitrary devices or as it says here, designated devices.

You probably do not have an enterprise in which to distribute the application, nor do you have a development team. Click Next.

## Select a Destination

You can either sign your app and create the bundle without uploading it to the App Store, or you can just go directly to the App Store, which is the default.

You are going to upload directly to App Store. Click Next.

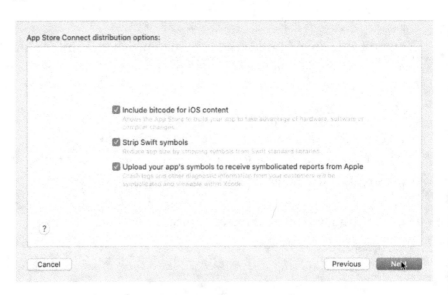

## App Store Connect Distribution Options

Again, you are going to take the defaults. All these options make sense for something you are going to distribute. Click Next.

## Application Signing

The next screen is about signing.

You are going to let Apple and XCode do all the hard work. I simply do not see the point in manually managing these things.

Maybe if you are part of a large organization, you might have a specific set of certificates that you have to use and device profiles.

This process is hard enough as it is. You want it to be as easy as possible and not make it any more difficult than necessary.

## Review App.ipa Content

At this point, everything is done; everything has been built. Now the only thing left is to upload it to the App Store Connect and it was successful. Click Upload.

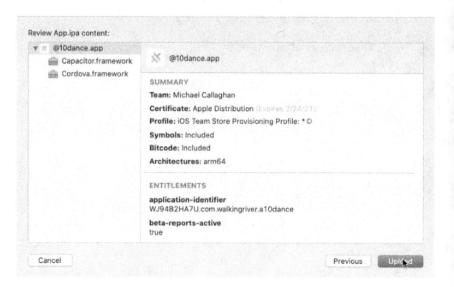

After a few minutes, assuming there were no errors, you should see this message indicating that the App was successfully uploaded to Apple.

# AppStore Connect Details

What do you need to do to get this thing in the App Store?

Log into https://appstoreconnect.apple.com and navigate to the App you just created in the last chapter. As you can see, it does not even have an icon yet.

That is fine for now, so go ahead and click on it and look at what you must do: supply a lot of images.

To me, the images are some of the hardest things to do because creating them is such a manual process.

I will show you how to get those images later. At this point, I want to help you get the rest of this form completed.

## Version Information

You must supply up to 170 seventy characters of promotional text. This is the first blurb of texts that your potential customers will see in the App Store. Think of it as a Tweet for your app. Be brief.

## Version Information

Promotional Text   ?

|  |
|  |
|  |

170

Description   ?

|  |
|  |
|  |

4,000

However, you have a lot more flexibility with the Description field. This is where you can have a lot of fun. This is where you want to tell the story of your application. You have up to 4000 characters to do so.

My recommendation is you spend a lot of time building this description. Think of it as the landing page for your application. You need to sell it. Why do people want to use your application?

Keywords   ?

|  |

100

Support URL   ?

http://example.com

Marketing URL   ?

http://example.com (optional)

Next, you can also supply up to 100 characters of keywords. There is an entire art to selecting keywords and there are Web sites devoted to the subject.

This URL should be a web page where can people go if they have questions about supporting the application.

Apple is going to require support URL when people have issues with your application. Apple will not offer support for your application. That is your job.

Next, you may optionally enter a marketing URL, which is a little bit different. This will be a URL that is visible in the App Store, which people can click on to find more information.

You must enter at least the support URL. You do not have to supply the marketing URL, but you probably should.

## App Clip

The app clip is a new feature from Apple in iOS 14. If you want to learn more about how it works, please see this URL: https://help.apple.com/app-store-connect/#/dev5b665db74.

## iMessage App

The app I built for this demo is not an iMessage App, so I will be skipping that one, too.

## Apple Watch App

This application that you are building now does not deal with the message app or the Apple Watch. As with the last two, you are going to skip those.

I am not suggesting that these are unimportant, but they are not relevant here.

## Build

As you scroll down, you get to the Build section.

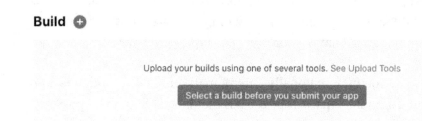

This is where you associate a build you just uploaded to the application being created on this page.

Uploading the application bundle to Apple is not instant, but it is quick. By the time you get here, it should have completed processing Click the big blue button to see a list of builds you have sent.

## Add Build

| BUILD | VERSION | HAS APP CLIP |
|-------|---------|--------------|
| ○ ⚒ 1 | 1.0 | NO |

In the screenshot above you can see I have uploaded a single build.
If you do not see any builds listed, but are sure you completed the
upload successfully, you probably need to wait a little longer.
Apple will email you when it has finished processing the upload.

Assuming you have one, select a build and click Done.

If you get a popup asking about encryption, Apple wants to know
if you are breaking any U.S. encryption export laws.

And as far as I know, at least for my demo app, it does not. You
need to ensure you answer honestly.

App Icon

## Build

| BUILD | VERSION | HAS APP CLIP |
|-------|---------|--------------|
|  1 | 1.0 | NO |

Included Assets

App Icon

The application icon, as you can see, is the default one from Capacitor. To fix that, you have to go back into Xcode and add the correct icons that you want and then upload a new build.

We will take care of that later.

# General App Information

You need to go through everything else on App Store Connect first.

**General App Information**

Version   ?

1.0

Copyright   ?

Age Rating   Edit
No Age Rating

Routing App Coverage File   ?

Choose File (Optional)

Here you need to give your app a version string, which should default to the one that corresponds to the build you selected.

Next, explain who owns the copyright. In other words, who owns the rights to the application? It should be you.

## Age Rating

Next, you need to help Apple calculate an age rating. You do that by clicking the Edit link and answering a massive list of questions.

This should be straightforward for you. Simply answer the questions honestly and let Apple do the rest.

The list is longer than the screenshot below, so make sure you scroll through the entire list.

**Edit Age Rating**

For each content description, select the level of frequency that best describes your app. The app's age rating that will appear on the App Store is the same across all of your platforms. It is based on the app's platform with the most mature rating.

Apps must not contain any obscene, pornographic, offensive, or defamatory or materials of any kind (text, graphics, images, photographs, and so on), or other content or materials that in Apple's reasonable judgement may be found objectionable.

| APPLE CONTENT DESCRIPTION | NONE | INFREQUENT/MILD | FREQUENT/INTENSE |
|---|---|---|---|
| Cartoon or Fantasy Violence | ○ | ○ | ○ |
| Realistic Violence | ○ | ○ | ○ |
| Prolonged Graphic or Sadistic Realistic Violence | ○ | ○ | ○ |
| Profanity or Crude Humor | ○ | ○ | ○ |
| Mature/Suggestive Themes | ○ | ○ | ○ |
| Horror/Fear Themes | ○ | ○ | ○ |
| Medical/Treatment Information | ○ | ○ | ○ |
| Alcohol, Tobacco, or Drug Use or References | ○ | ○ | ○ |
| Simulated Gambling | ○ | ○ | ○ |
| Sexual Content or Nudity | ○ | ○ | ○ |

Cancel   Done

Here is the complete list, as of the time I am writing this:

- Cartoon or Fantasy Violence
- Realistic Violence
- Prolonged Graphic or Sadistic Realistic Violence
- Profanity or Crude Humor
- Mature/Suggestive Themes
- Horror/Fear Themes
- Medical/Treatment Information
- Alcohol, Tobacco, or Drug Use or References
- Simulated Gambling
- Sexual Content or Nudity

- Graphic Sexual Content and Nudity
- Unrestricted Web Access
- Gambling and Contests
- Made for Kids (Requires an age recommendation)

Once you answer those questions, Apple then applies a rating.

## Game Center

If your app is a game, click the Game Center checkbox. You may need to supply more information about your game's multiplayer compatibility, which is beyond the scope of this writing.

## App Review Information

This next section is additional information for the reviewer, the human who's going to review your application.

**App Review Information**

Sign-In Information  ?
Provide a user name and password so we can sign in to
your app. We'll need this to complete your app review.

Contact Information  ?

| First name | Last name |

☑ Sign-in required

| Phone number | Email |

| User name | Password |

Notes  ?

Do they need to sign in to use the app? If so, check the "Sign-in required" box and supply a username and password that will let them log into the app.

This is an important thing to pay attention to because it is possible that your app might be password protected. If that is not the case, leave it unchecked.

Contact information is pretty straightforward. Although I have never had it happen, you should give them enough information to contact you in case they have questions.

## Notes

The notes box is for any other information you think the reviewer might need to help with the review. Personally, I have always left it blank.

## Attachment

If your application is complicated enough, you may attach documentation or videos or other type of help to make it easier for the person who is reviewing it to understand how to use your application.

## Version Release

When do you want them to release the application to the public?

- You can manually do it.
- You can automatically do it, which is the default.
- Or you can specify a date, and Apple will note release before this particular date and time.

## Advertising Identifier

And then finally, advertising. Does your application use ads? In other words, does it display ads? I found out the hard way a long time ago, that if you use Google AdSense, that counts as a yes.

And if you tell them no, and your application really does it will get rejected.

If you select Yes, a few more options appear. If you are going to serve ads, but you are not going to link apps together so that the advertisements, can be related. I believe that is what the second one is.

Personally, I have never done anything other than simply serving ads from AdSense, and I have never checked the second and third boxes.

## Limit Ad Tracking setting in iOS

You must click the final checkbox or you cannot continue.

However, make sure you look at that red text. If you answer the questions incorrectly and they find out about it, Apple will reject your app, remove it from the apps or issue a warning.

And if you do it again, they may ban your account entirely.

Save everything now, but do not try to submit it for review just yet. You still need to take care of the icons, splash screen, and screenshots.

We will do that over the next two chapters.

# App Icons and Splash Screen

Now it is time get the application icon and splash screen taken care of. It is not hard to do, and I will show you a straightforward way to handle it.

Back in the pre-Capacitor days when everyone was using Cordova, Cordova had a command line option to generate icons and splash screens from a source image.

These days, I am trying to stay away from any of the Cordova tools, because Capacitor is the future.

## Cordova-Res

The tool you are going to use is called cordova-res, which you can see at https://github.com/ionic-team/cordova-res.

It is a tool from the Ionic team that replicates the functionality that the Cordova command line used to provide.

The bonus is that it does it all locally rather than sending the file out to the Web.

I have a feeling they are going to rename it soon and get rid of the word "cordova" in its name.

## Default Images

Take a look at the screenshot below.

What you have on the left is a resources folder that is just inside your project root folder. This is where the source images are going to live.

On the right, you can see the iPhone simulator is running with the default Capacitor icon visible.

And if you were to launch the application, you would quickly see the splash screen.

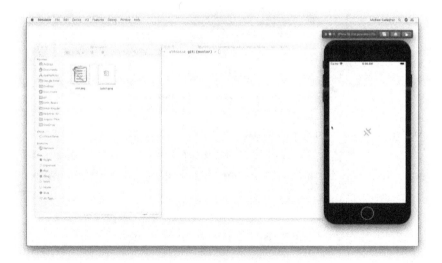

The default splash screen is just a white image with the Capacitor logo in the middle. That seems to be the case for a lot of iOS apps, so you are going to stick to that for the purposes of this demo.

# Icon Image

To find my icon, I downloaded a PNG file from
https://pixabay.com, an archive of more than a million images that
are free to use for almost any purpose. It is simply a clipboard with
a checklist and pencil.

Apple highly recommends not using transparency in your icons.

And if you look at the icons that are visible in the simulator, you
can see what happens.

The files and @10dance icons all have white backgrounds, but most icons in iOS seem not to do that.

For the most part, you want your icon to be the color that you expect it to be. What will happen is because you are using a PNG file with transparency, those transparent areas will be turned white. I am OK with that if you are.

## Splash Screen Image

And the splash screen is similar. It is the same exact image centered within a much larger image. The image size is 2732 x 2732, which is the recommended or required size.

Stay in the command line for now. Once you have your favorite terminal or shell ready, go ahead and install the package as a development dependency for this project.

```
npm install -D cordova-res
```

The -D flag installs the package as a development dependency. This means it will be available to your project at build time, but it will not ship with the application. This is exactly what we want.

Next, you are going to tell Cordova Res to build the images you need. You can execute it with simple npx command:

```
npx cordova-res ios --skip-conf --copy
```

The first part of the command, npx, allows you to execute an npm package that is only installed locally.

"cordova-res" is the actual command name.

"ios" indicates to build an icon and splash screen only for an iOS project. You can also specify "android" but you probably do not want to do that just now.

Because you do have a config file, which is part of a Cordova application, specify the "--skip-config" flag.

Finally, "--copy" instructs the command to copy the resulting resources into your Xcode project.

You are likely to see some warnings, but otherwise it should run quickly.

## Generated Icons

If you look in the ./ios/icon folder, you should see almost 30 generated icons of various sizes.

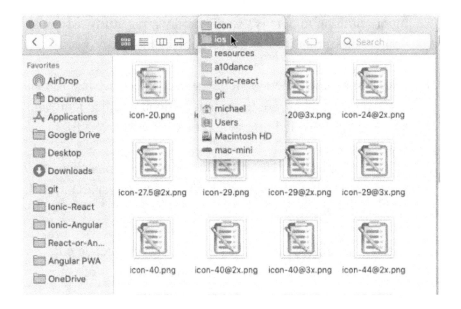

## Generated Splash Screens

It also created the splash screen for you in multiple sizes. You can find those in the ./ios/splash folder.

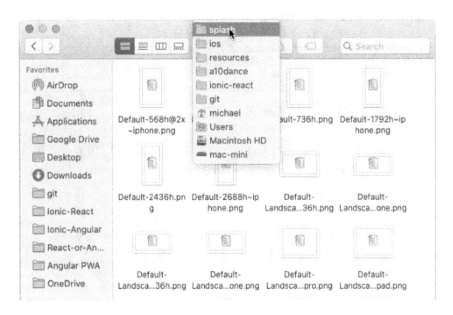

An important thing to note is that the cordova-res utility assumes that you are executing it from the root folder of your project.

It further assumes that the icon in the splash screen are in a folder called Resources at that root level, that the icon is called icon, and the splash screen is called Splash and they are both PNG files.

You may see a warning that because there was an alpha channel, which means there was transparency, that all the transparency will be filled in with white.

Personally, I am fine with that. If you are not, you need to edit your images to replace the transparency with the color of your choice.

## Using the New Images

To see how it looks and the changes that were made, you simply need to open the Xcode project, which you can you can do with the following handy command.

```
npx cap open ios
```

That will launch Xcode for you.

At this point, all you need to do is execute the application and let it deploy to the simulator. Xcode should have already picked up all the new assets for you.

Pay close attention to the simulator screen after you press play. You should see the icon change and then the splash screen should appear.

## Upload New Build

You still need to upload this version of the code to the App Store, but that is the exact same process you saw a few chapters ago. I will not go through that again here.

# Screenshots and Final Submission

The very last thing you need to do now to submit the application to the App Store officially is to provide some screenshots at various resolutions.

I am going to take a little bit of a detour here. There really is no point in submitting my demo app as it now stands to Apple. It does not really do anything, and Apple will not approve anything like that.

To help me get my point across and show exactly how this is done, I am going to submit an update to an existing application.

I will show you how you create the screenshots.

Then I will show you a completed App Store submission and show how to submit an update.

All these things working together I think will be important for you in the future with your own applications.

## Park Pursuit

Here is my application, known as Park Pursuit. If you would like to follow along, please visit https://park-pursuit.com and select the appropriate store from which to download the app.

It is a visual scavenger hunt with geolocation built into it.

It is itself an Ionic app, and it uses Capacitor, so it is everything you may have seen so far in my books and courses.

On the right in the picture above, you can see the iPhone 11 Pro Max running in the iOS Simulator. Apple wants screenshots of various sizes, and this phone is one of them.

This is the bare minimum as I am writing this book. You must supply images from a 6.5-inch iPhone display and a 5.5-inch iPhone display.

Plus, because this application supports iPads, you must also supply screenshots for an iPad Pro, both second and third generation.

You can supply images for every possible screen size, but it is not strictly necessary. The App Store is OK with that and will use the larger screenshots in place of the smaller devices.

You can see that it is using the 12.9-inch display for the iPad. For some of the smaller iPhone models, it uses the larger screenshots and simply scales down.

I do need to replace a few of these. One of the existing screenshots shows the theme parks available to play for the scavenger hunt. I now provide more theme parks, so I want to upload the new screenshot to show that change.

## App Demo

Here is a quick look at the App back in Xcode. When I launch it in the simulator, you can see its custom splash screen.

The app starts with the instruction screen.

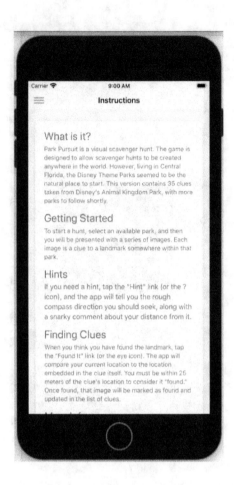

At that point, the user can choose to start a new game.

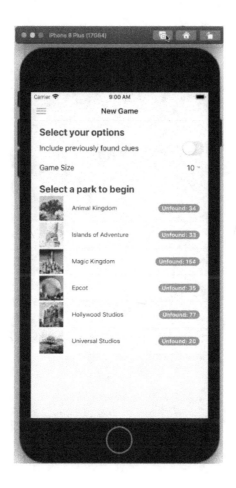

The first thing you need to do with the new game is to tell Park Pursuit what theme park you are visiting.

Let us imagine you are visiting Universal Studios and there are only 20 clues.

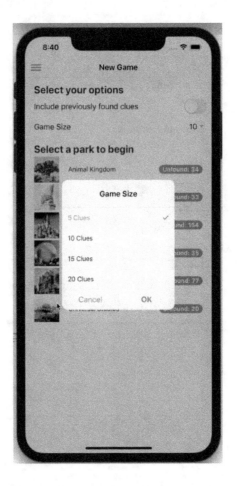

The player might select a short game of five clues. When they then click the theme park, it immediately selects five random clues from the 20 that it has and displays them in the game screen.

The object of the game is to look for these hidden details or these small details as you visit the theme parks.

When you think you found one, you can select it to see a slightly larger image. This screen also allows you to tell the game you think you have found the clue shown.

Tapping the image flips the card to reveal a hint on the back along with a button that says "Found It."

The game is GPS-aware. It calculates the distance between where the image was taken and the current location of your mobile device. It allows a match if the two are within approximately ten meters from each other.

You can try to play it from a distance greater than that, but if you tell it you found a clue, it is not going to believe you.

In this case, it asks whether you are even in the same park. I am about a dozen miles from this park, and the game knows it. Quite frankly, that is the behavior I want.

## Create the Screenshots

Going back to the New Game screen, this is the primary screenshot I want to replace. You are free to upload as many as ten screenshots of any part of your app that you feel will help sell it. Choose wisely.

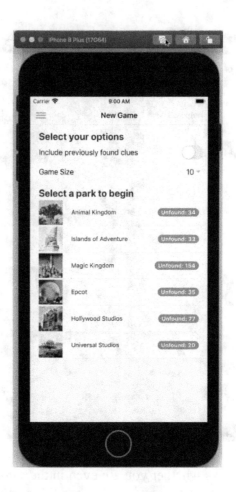

I can take that screenshot in any one of three ways: Select the File |
Save Screen menu, Click the camera icon in the simulator
window's title bar, or simply type Cmd + S.

By default, the screenshot is saved on the Desktop, with the name
being Simulator Screen Shot, the name of simulator's loaded
device, followed by a date and time stamp.

At the absolute minimum, the App Store is going to require screenshots at three different resolutions. At the time of this writing, the way to get those sizes is to use these iPhone models (either real devices or in the simulator):

| APP STORE CONNECT | SIMULATOR DEVICE |
| --- | --- |
| iPhone 6.5" Display | iPhone 11 Pro Max |
| iPhone 5.5" Display | iPhone 8 Plus |
| iPad Pro 12.9" (3$^{rd}$ Generation) | iPad Pro 12.9" (4$^{th}$ Generation) |

If you are following along, go ahead and make your screenshots for each of these devices and set them aside for a few moments.

## Submit a New Build

When anything in your application changes, you need to submit a new build to Apple. If you are simply following along and want to get straight to the screenshots, you can skip this part. I am including it here for completeness.

To submit a new build, the important thing to recall is that the command to start this process is the menu Product | Archive. Do not forget that you cannot start an archive while you have a simulator selected. You must either select a real iPhone that is currently connected to your Mac, or a Generic Device.

In my case, I usually select my real iPhone.

That allows me to archive.

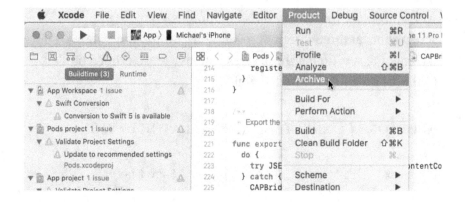

It is worth pointing out that I bumped the version number in Xcode, this should create a brand new build and should automatically submit it to App Store Connect for me.

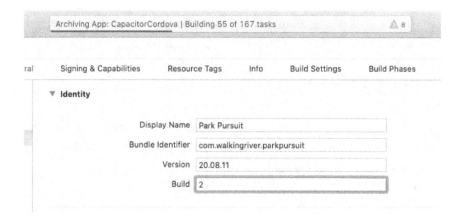

Once the app is uploaded, you can return to Safari.

It created a new version, but that version is not reflected yet in the App Store. You can clearly see that the version strings do not match.

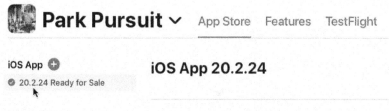

## iOS App 20.2.24

**Version Information**

This version, 20.2.24, tells me that I have not released since February 24, 2020. This is how I have been versioning, by the date the app was released.

# Create a New Version

To release the build I just uploaded, I need to tell it I want a new version, so I click the plus here.

The first thing Apple wants to know for a new version is what the new version should be

Then I need to tell it what has changed since the last version.

# iOS App 20.08.11

## Version Information

What's New in This Version  ?

Now playable in all six major Central Florida theme parks, including all four Disney Parks and both Universal Orlando parks! All ads have been removed.

I added more theme parks and removed all ads. That is enough detail.

Next, I need to replace the outdated screenshots with some new ones. I already have 10 of the maximum10 screenshots, so I have to delete one for each new one I want to add.

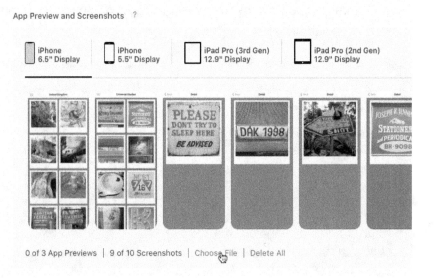

App Preview and Screenshots  ?

iPhone 6.5" Display     iPhone 5.5" Display     iPad Pro (3rd Gen) 12.9" Display     iPad Pro (2nd Gen) 12.9" Display

0 of 3 App Previews  |  9 of 10 Screenshots  |  Choose File  |  Delete All

I want to add the one I just captured, which shows the New Game screen with the additional theme parks. You can select images from your computer or simply drag them into this window.

Once uploaded, you can drag the images around to order them however you think makes sense. I usually put them in the same order a player would likely encounter them.

Let me show you what happens if you try to drag a file the wrong size so you know you what it will do.

If try to drag a file from the wrong iPhone, it complains with a pretty obvious error.

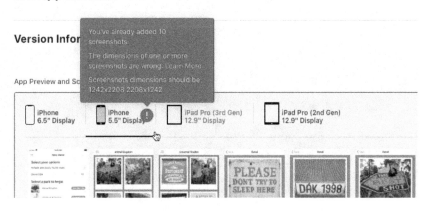

It will not allow it because the dimensions are wrong, which means you need to go back into Xcode and the simulator. If you have not yet done so, you need to provide it with an 8 Plus screen for a 5.5" Display.

Once you have completed the iPhone screens, you still need to upload images for an iPad pro and an iPad pro second edition.

This is simply repeating the same process over for these.

I think it is pretty straightforward from here, that you can create the screenshots, and now you know where to put them.

# Final Submission

Once your screenshots are all there, it is time to finish the submission.

In my case, I need to scroll down and tell the App Store that the application no longer provides advertising. It should be safe to select no here.

## Advertising Identifier

Does this app use the Advertising Identifier (IDFA)?

○ Yes, my app uses an IDFA

◉ No, it doesn't

The Advertising Identifier (IDFA) is a unique ID for each iOS d

The next thing to do is to provide some promotional text.

Promotional Text

> Park Pursuit is a visual scavenger hunt that you can play on your phone in all six major Central Florida theme parks. Search for clues and challenge your friends today!

Finally, it is time to select a build.

Upload your builds using one of several tools. See Upload Tools

Select a build before you submit your app.

This is the one you just uploaded, and you can see it is missing a compliance, but you'll show you what you need to do next.

## Add Build

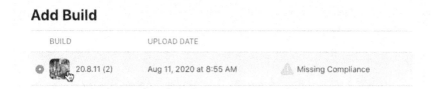

Essentially, it wants to make sure that you are allowed to export the application from the United States, and so it wants to know if you are using an encryption that's trade restricted.

Be careful with this one. You do not want to answer it incorrectly. In my case, I am not using any encryption.

## Export Compliance Information

Does your app use encryption? Select Yes even if your app only uses the standard encryption within Apple's operating system.

○ Yes

◉ No

(i) It is your responsibility to comply with export regulations, and you should revisit these questions if your encryption or exemption status changes. If your encryption and exemption eligibility stay the same, specify this in the target properties table in Xcode. Learn More

**App Uses Non-Exempt Encryption : No**

(i) If you are making use of ATS or making a call to HTTPS, you are required to submit a year-end self classification report to the US government. Learn More

Export laws require that products containing encryption must be properly authorized for export. Failure to comply could result in severe penalties. Learn More

Set Up Later    Done

You can see what would happen if you said yes, then you would have to go through some other steps, but as I said, I am not doing that. I am not using any encryption.

## Export Compliance Information

Does your app use encryption? Select Yes even if your app only uses the standard encryption within Apple's operating system.

◉ Yes

○ No

Export laws require that products containing encryption must be properly authorized for export. Failure to comply could result in severe penalties. Learn More

Select the appropriate answer for the app, assuming you are following along. Then you can save.

And finally, you can submit the application for review.

## The Review Process

And now, as with all things Appstore, you wait.

Your worst-case scenario is it gets rejected entirely. Unfortunately, I have had a number of those that have done that.

Your best case scenario, and what you should expect to happen, is that it will be approved relatively quickly.

This is the progression of emails you should expect after you submit your app to the App Store.

## Completed Processing

This first one indicates that the that you uploaded has completed processing. You need to wait for that to finish before you can select it as your build.

**App Store Connect**

Dear Michael Callaghan10686145711,

The following build has completed processing:

Platform: iOS
App Name: Park Pursuit
Build Number: 2
Version Number: 20.8.11
App SKU: park-pursuit
App Apple ID: 1335800270

You can now use this build for TestFlight testing or submit it to the App Store.

If you have any questions regarding your app, click Contact Us in App Store Connect.

Regards,

The App Store team

Contact Us I App Store Connect I One Apple Park Way, Cupertino, CA 95014

Privacy Policy I Terms of Service

## Waiting for Review

A few minutes later, after clicking submit for approval, I received this email telling me that the application is now waiting for review.

This means it is in the queue, but not yet assigned to a person.

**App Store Connect**

Dear Michael Callaghan|10686145711,

The status of your app has changed to **Waiting for Review**.

App Name: Park Pursuit
App Version Number: 20.08.11
App SKU: park-pursuit
App Apple ID: 1335800270

To make changes to this app, go to your apps's page in My Apps in App Store Connect.

If you have any questions, contact us.

Best regards,
The App Store Team

Contact Us | App Store Connect | One Apple Park Way, Cupertino, CA 95014

Privacy Policy | Terms of Service

## In Review

Almost eight hours later, I received the email telling me that the app is now in review by a person at Apple.

**App Store Connect**

Dear Michael Callaghan|1068614571|1,

The status of your app has changed to **In Review.**

App Name: Park Pursuit
App Version Number: 20.08.11
App SKU: park-pursuit
App Apple ID: 1335800270

To make changes to this app, go to your apps's page in My Apps in App Store Connect.

If you have any questions, contact us.

Best regards,
The App Store Team

## Available for Sale

Finally, about three hours after that, I received this email letting me know that my application has been approved and is now available for sale on the App Store.

## App Store Connect

Dear Michael Callaghan!10686145711,

The following app has been approved for the App Store:

App Name: Park Pursuit⊕
App Version Number: 20.08.11
App Type: iOS
App SKU: park-pursuit
App Apple ID: 1335800270

For details on marketing your app, including information on using the App Store badge and Apple product images, messaging and writing style, legal requirements, and more, read the App Store Marketing Guidelines.

If you have any questions, contact us.

Best regards,
App Store Review

Total elapsed time from submission to approval: just under 11 hours.

Do not get too discouraged if you hear nothing for hours at a time, especially if you are submitting a brand new app.

I think my first one took almost a week to get approved.

# Wrap Up

Congratulations! In this book, you managed to build an App Store version of a web application using Ionic's Capacitor.

You saw the application run on a real device and on the iOS simulator.

Then you successfully created and uploaded the application to Apple's App Store Connect.

You created some custom icons and splash screens, making the app look more normal, more natural.

You used the iOS Simulator to create the required App Store screenshots at various resolutions.

And finally, if all went well, you submitted the app to the App Store for approval.

If you have been following along, you should now have everything you need to get your own application submitted to the App Store and hopefully approved.

# What Next?

I hope you enjoyed this overview of deploying a web application to the Apple App Store. If so, please consider leaving me a positive review at the seller's site where you purchased it. Also consider some of my other titles.

You can always checkout my other offerings at https://walkingriver.gumroad.com.

Please follow me at Twitter for regular updates. My handle is @walkingriver.

www.ingramcontent.com/pod-product-compliance
Lightning Source LLC
LaVergne TN
LVHW051605050326
832903LV00033B/4374